Counting in the Grasslands 1-2-3

Aaron R. Murray

Enslow Elementary

an imprint of

Enslow Publishers, Inc.

40 Industrial Road
Box 398
Berkeley Heights, NJ 07922
USA

http://www.enslow.com

Enslow Elementary, an imprint of Enslow Publishers, Inc.
Enslow Elementary® is a registered trademark of Enslow Publishers, Inc.

Library of Congress Cataloging-in-Publication Data

Murray, Aaron R.
  Counting in the grasslands 1-2-3 / Aaron Murray.
    p. cm. — (All about counting in the biomes)
  Includes index.
  Summary: "Introduces pre-readers to simple concepts about the grasslands using short sentences and
repetition of words"—Provided by publisher.
  ISBN 978-0-7660-4054-0
  1. Grasslands—Juvenile literature. 2. Counting—Juvenile literature. I. Title.
  QH87.7.M86 2012
  333.74—dc23
                              2011037460

Future editions:
Paperback ISBN 978-1-4644-0060-5
ePUB ISBN 978-1-4645-0967-4
PDF ISBN 978-1-4646-0967-1

Printed in the United States of America

032012 Lake Book Manufacturing, Inc., Melrose Park, IL

10 9 8 7 6 5 4 3 2 1

To Our Readers: We have done our best to make sure all Internet Addresses in this book were active
and appropriate when we went to press. However, the author and the publisher have no control over and
assume no liability for the material available on those Internet sites or on other Web sites they may link
to. Any comments or suggestions can be sent by e-mail to comments@enslow.com or to the address on
the back cover.

♻ Enslow Publishers, Inc., is committed to printing our books on recycled paper. The paper in every
book contains 10% to 30% post-consumer waste (PCW). The cover board on the outside of each book
contains 100% PCW. Our goal is to do our part to help young people and the environment too!

Photo Credits: © iStockphoto.com/Chad Davis, pp. 3 (prairie dog), 6; Photos.com: Jupiterimages, pp.
3 (zebra), 14; Michael Steden, p. 10, Peter Zurek, p. 8; Shutterstock.com, pp, 1, 3 (bison, zebra), 4, 12,
16, 18, 20, 22.

Cover Photo: Shutterstock.com

Note to Parents and Teachers
Help pre-readers get a jump start on reading. These lively stories introduce simple concepts with
repetition of words and short simple sentences. Photos and illustrations fill the pages with color and
effectively enhance the text. Free Educator Guides are available for this series at www.enslow.com.
Search for the *All About Counting in the Biomes* series name.

Contents

Words to Know

bison   **prairie dog**   **zebra**

Monarch
butterfly

Let's count!

1

One butterfly

Two prairie dogs

Ostriches

Three heads

Lion

4 Four paws

Five elephants

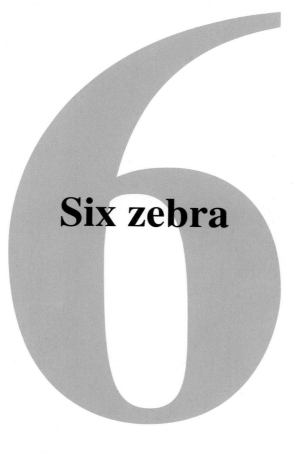

Six zebra

Black-eyed
Susans

Seven flowers

Eight giraffe

Mustangs

Nine horses

10

Ten bison

Read More

Anderson, Sheila. *What Can Live in a Grassland?* Minneapolis, Minn.: Lerner Classroom, 2010.

Bullock, Linda. *Living in the Savannah*. Danbury, Conn.: Children's Press, 2004.

MacAulay, Kelley. *A Grassland Habitat*. New York: Crabtree, 2006.

Web Sites

Kids Do Ecology: Savanna
<http://kids.nceas.ucsb.edu/biomes/savanna.html>

Missouri Botanical Garden: Biomes of the World: Grasslands
<http://www.mbgnet.net/sets/grasslnd/index.htm>

National Geographic Kids: South African Wildlife
<http://kids.nationalgeographic.com/kids/photos/south-african-wildlife/>

Index

Guided Reading Level: A
Guided Reading Leveling System is based on the guidelines recommended by Fountas and Pinnell.

Word Count: 23